'Who am I impersonating today? Which face do I wish to show to the world? Under what mask do I want to hide?' Inge Morath and Saul Steinberg

‘I have never pretended to be someone else, just sometimes a different me’

Laura Unsworth, Member of Manchester Art Gallery’s Creative Consultants Youth Board

This guide accompanies the exhibition *Disguise* at Manchester Art Gallery **12 February - 6 June 2004** Artists: Leigh Bowery and Fergus Greer, Claude Cahun, Marcus Coates, Laura Ford, Nikki S Lee, Kenny Macleod, Inge Morath and Saul Steinberg, Yasumasa Morimura, Cindy Sherman, Gillian Wearing

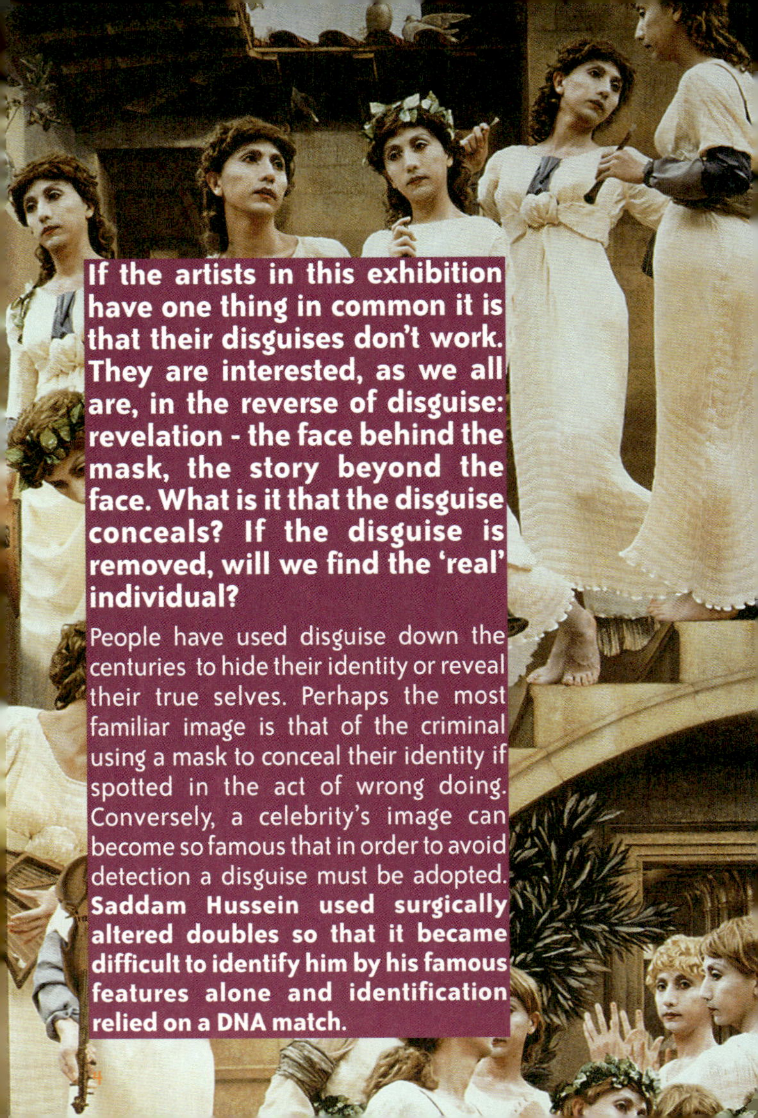

If the artists in this exhibition have one thing in common it is that their disguises don't work. They are interested, as we all are, in the reverse of disguise: revelation - the face behind the mask, the story beyond the face. What is it that the disguise conceals? If the disguise is removed, will we find the 'real' individual?

People have used disguise down the centuries to hide their identity or reveal their true selves. Perhaps the most familiar image is that of the criminal using a mask to conceal their identity if spotted in the act of wrong doing. Conversely, a celebrity's image can become so famous that in order to avoid detection a disguise must be adopted. **Saddam Hussein used surgically altered doubles so that it became difficult to identify him by his famous features alone and identification relied on a DNA match.**

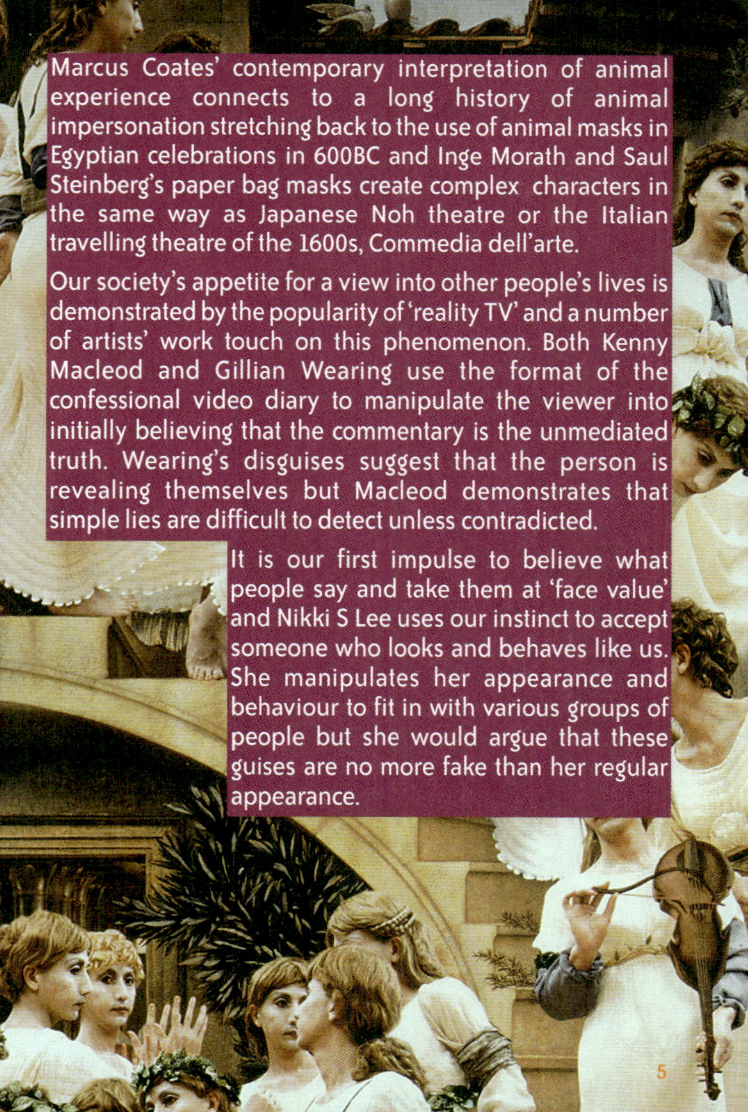

Marcus Coates' contemporary interpretation of animal experience connects to a long history of animal impersonation stretching back to the use of animal masks in Egyptian celebrations in 600BC and Inge Morath and Saul Steinberg's paper bag masks create complex characters in the same way as Japanese Noh theatre or the Italian travelling theatre of the 1600s, Commedia dell'arte.

Our society's appetite for a view into other people's lives is demonstrated by the popularity of 'reality TV' and a number of artists' work touch on this phenomenon. Both Kenny Macleod and Gillian Wearing use the format of the confessional video diary to manipulate the viewer into initially believing that the commentary is the unmediated truth. Wearing's disguises suggest that the person is revealing themselves but Macleod demonstrates that simple lies are difficult to detect unless contradicted.

It is our first impulse to believe what people say and take them at 'face value' and Nikki S Lee uses our instinct to accept someone who looks and behaves like us. She manipulates her appearance and behaviour to fit in with various groups of people but she would argue that these guises are no more fake than her regular appearance.

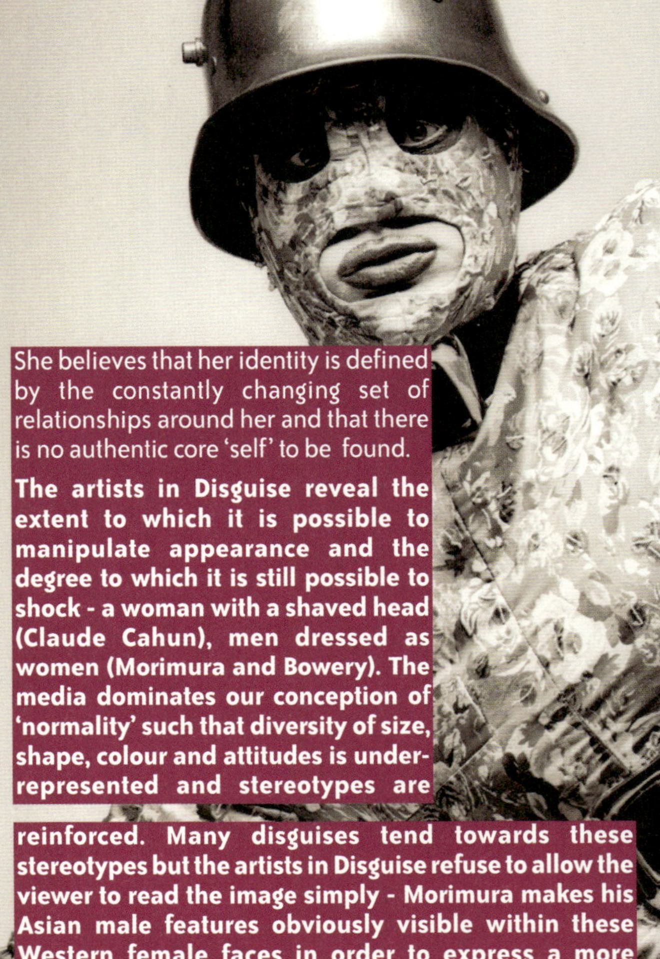

She believes that her identity is defined by the constantly changing set of relationships around her and that there is no authentic core 'self' to be found.

The artists in Disguise reveal the extent to which it is possible to manipulate appearance and the degree to which it is still possible to shock - a woman with a shaved head (Claude Cahun), men dressed as women (Morimura and Bowery). The media dominates our conception of 'normality' such that diversity of size, shape, colour and attitudes is under-represented and stereotypes are reinforced. Many disguises tend towards these stereotypes but the artists in Disguise refuse to allow the viewer to read the image simply - Morimura makes his Asian male features obviously visible within these Western female faces in order to express a more

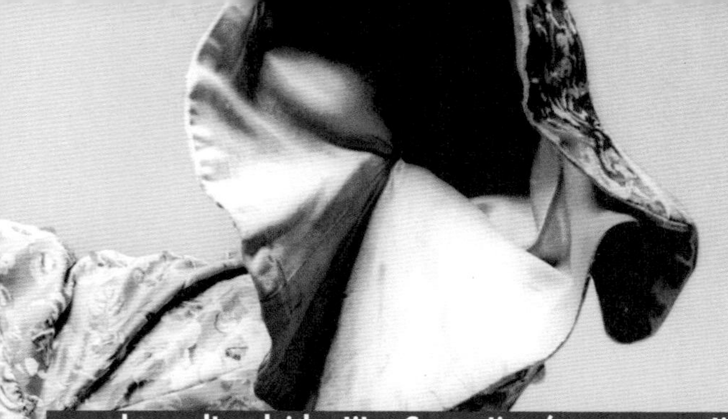

complex cultural identity. Cosmetics (even cosmetic surgery) may offer the opportunity to achieve the media ideal of youth and beauty but Sherman's images show women who make a game attempt but ultimately fail.

We live in a society which largely allows free expression of speech and appearance but many of us make fairly conventional choices when presenting ourselves to the world. As a result those who digress from the norm attract attention and those who blend in may be ignored, despite concealing an interesting story.

You can't tell a book by its cover but a careful look at someone's choice of disguise can reveal more than the face it conceals.

Catherine Dickinson
Curator (Exhibitions and Displays)
Manchester Art Gallery

Image: Leigh Bowery and Fergus Greer, *Session IV/ Look 23/ August 1991* Lightjet photographic prints, mounted on aluminium, Collection of Fergus Greer, Courtesy of The Michael Hoppen Gallery

'Who am I impersonating today? Which face do I wish to show to the world? Under what mask do I want to hide?' Inge Morath and Saul Steinberg

The first time Inge Morath knocked on Saul Steinberg's door in New York he answered wearing a mask drawn onto a grocery bag. From that moment in 1959 they worked together to create a series of satirical images of New York high society.

Morath's deadpan black and white photographic style gives Steinberg's whimsical characters a gravity and longevity. Steinberg is more commonly known for his drawings in the New Yorker and Morath for her work with Magnum Photos and as Henri Cartier-Bresson's assistant

'I always had a passion for taking portraits, but here, an encounter of a different kind had taken place: the person sitting for the portrait wore a mask, impersonating an archetype. We discussed techniques of impersonating someone else...like those delicious moments during trips when no one knows you and you can present a new persona for a while.' Inge Morath.

Inge Morath was born in 1923 in Austria and died in 2002

Saul Steinberg was born in 1914 USA and died in 1999

Image:
USA, 1961,
photograph by Inge Morath ©The Estate of Inge Morath /MAGNUM, Mask by Saul Steinberg © The Saul Steinberg Foundation/ARS, NY
Black and white resin print

Inge Morath and Saul Steinberg

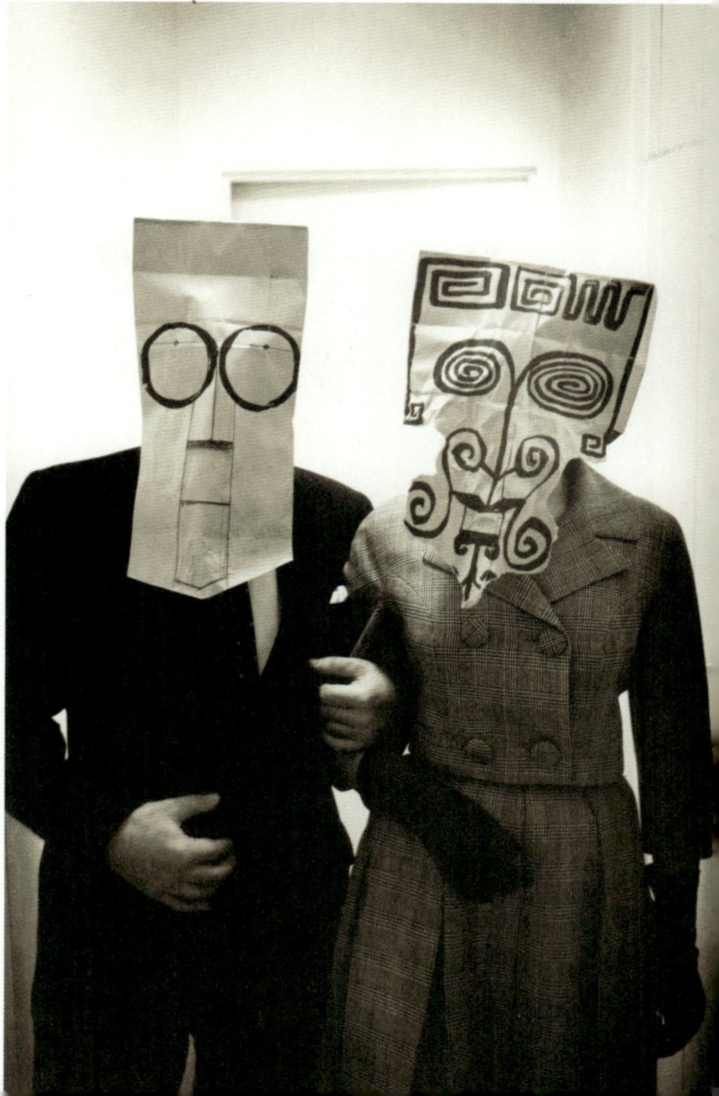

Leigh Bowery and Fergus Greer

As a tall, bald, bulky man Bowery's disguises had to be elaborate. He hid his masculinity with a fantasy femininity, creating grotesque and comical parodies of the human silhouette. Bowery was a celebrity within the 1980s London club scene and each costume was created for a night out. These performances were transient but a record of his art lies in the photographs he and photographer Fergus Greer created during 1988 - 1994. Greer's studio - style portraits recall and revolutionise both classical portraiture and contemporary fashion images.

Bowery's extraordinary costumes challenge our ideas about the ideal body shape. Those who witnessed his performances describe how his huge stature in costume contributed to the power and magnetism of his creations. Bowery's relatively simple changes in body silhouette seem shocking compared to the narrow definition of male and female beauty promoted by the media.

The exhibition features a number of gay artists who have used disguises to express the complexity of their feelings about their identity. Bowery's art was a continual self exploration and self invention. He loved the attention attracted by his appearance and exploited the liberating effect of disguise to behave outrageously.

Leigh Bowery was born in Australia in 1961 and died in 1994

Fergus Greer was born in Aldershot in 1964 and now lives in Los Angeles

Image:
Leigh Bowery and Fergus Greer, *Session II/Look 9/July 1989*
Lightjet photographic prints, mounted on aluminium, Collection of Fergus Greer, Courtesy of The Michael Hoppen Gallery

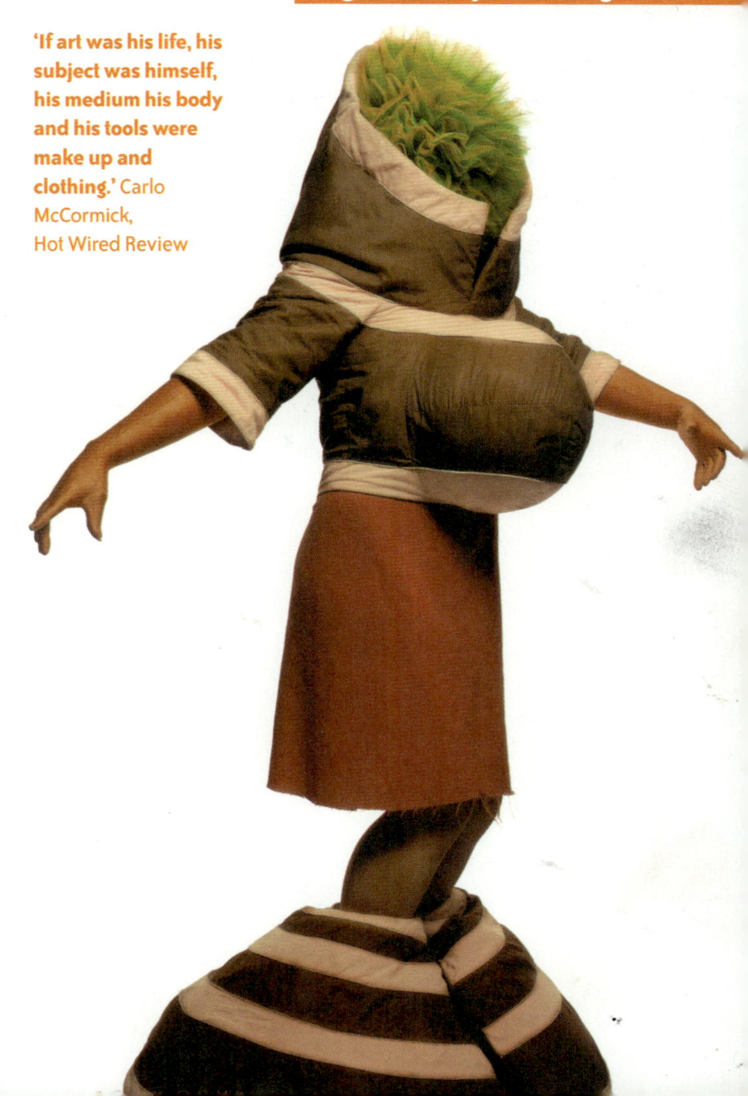

'If art was his life, his subject was himself, his medium his body and his tools were make up and clothing.' Carlo McCormick, Hot Wired Review

'The very concealment of the identity of the faceless boys lends the work its enigmatic allure and seems to invite or demand intense affectionate engagement' from *The Great Indoors* David Lomas from *Laura Ford* published by Centro deArte de Salamanca

Laura Ford was born in Wales in 1961 and now lives in London

Laura Ford

Despite an absence of facial features, the character, emotions and predicament of Laura Ford's individuals are clearly articulated. The ineffectiveness of their disguise is touching - boys encumbered with huge trunk-like noses that are impossible to conceal - small girls up to no good but betrayed by their pretty dresses. Their anonymity does nothing to conceal their outrageous actions as they are caught attempting to perform tasks that seem way beyond their capabilities.

Laura Ford has created two new site specific sculptures in the neo-classical entrance hall to Manchester Art Gallery called *Some Mothers' Sons 2* and *3*. They are sited on twin plinths either side of the main staircase where you might expect to find classical sculpture or elaborate floral displays to accompany civic or corporate events. Ford's works combine both of these elements. Her anonymous child-size military figures are bent on one knee in a classical, heroic, obedient pose - appropriate to the images of war depicted in the casts of the Parthenon Frieze above them. But these small figures seem at odds with their situation. Their disproportionately large backpacks act as planters for camouflage foliage more appropriate to an office than a battlefield.

Image: Laura Ford
Chintz Girl 1998
plaster, wire, fabric
Courtesy Mimi Floback

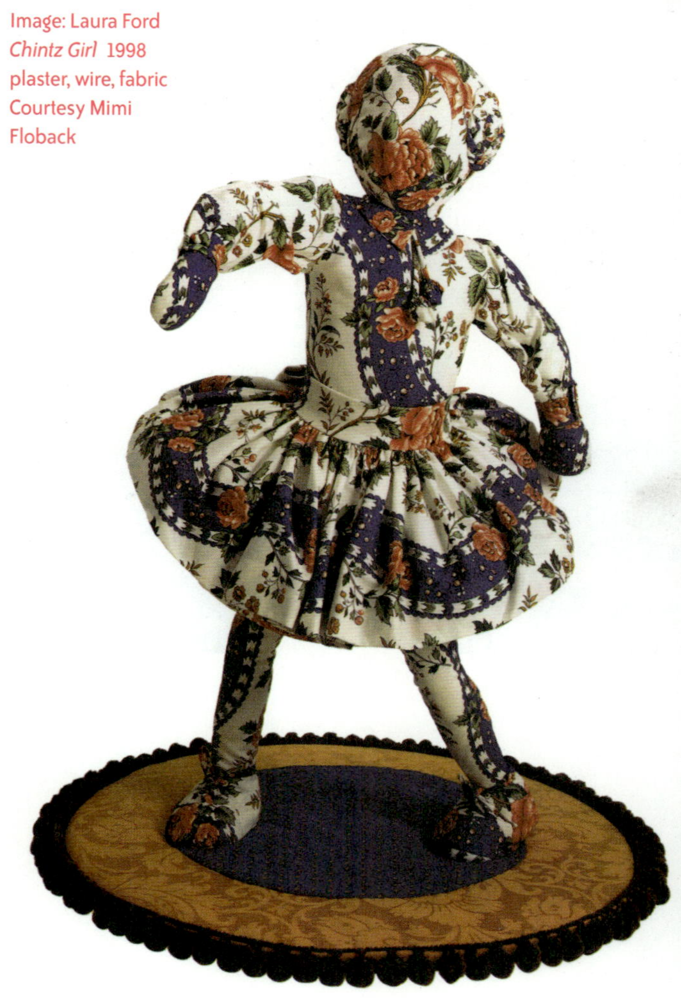

Marcus Coates

'He investigates humanness by experimenting with peregrineness, deerness, foxness' Tracey Warr in *Marcus Coates* published by Grizedale Books

Marcus Coates is interested in finding out what it is like to be an animal. By re-enacting their behaviour, habits and experiences he attempts to understand their experience of self and compare it to that of being human. His artworks document this process of physical and psychological adaptation - often a failed experiment

Finfolk (2003) is based on a traditional tale from Northern Scotland, Iceland and Norway. Finfolk or Selkies are seals that come ashore in human form, they are often held responsible for creating storms, unaccountable pregnancies and disappearances.

Born in 1968 in Edgware and now lives in Berwick-upon-Tweed

Images:
Marcus Coates
Finfolk, 2003
DVD 7 mins
Courtesy the artist
Photo: Mark Pinder
page 17 Marcus Coates
Local Birds, 2001
DVD 9mins
Courtesy the artist

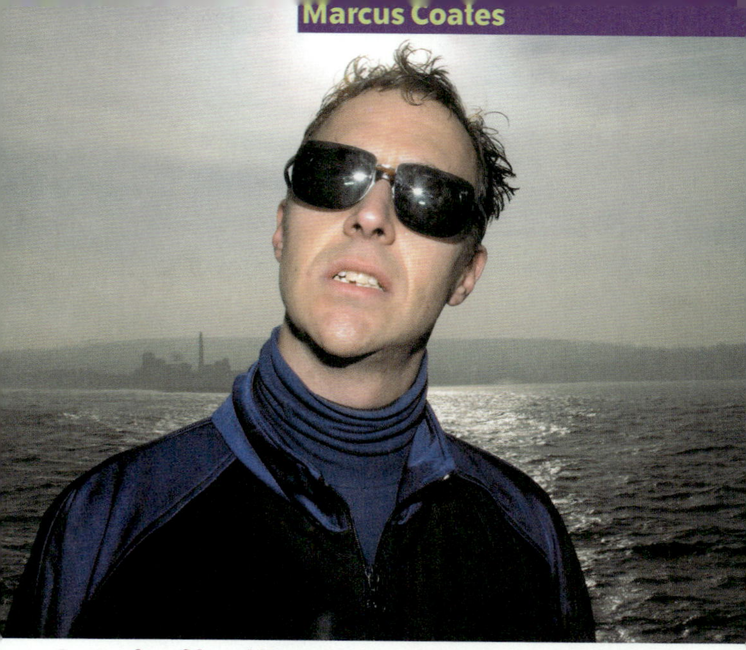

Coates has filmed himself as a contemporary Selkie, climbing out of the swirling North Sea up onto the quayside. As he strolls up and down dressed in an Adidas shellsuit and trainers, he engages us in a monologue peppered with expletives and aggression - an invented language as presumably a seal's speech would not be familiar to us. There is something disappointingly ordinary and parochial about this mythical being. As he climbs back down into the dark waters and disappears we are left feeling cheated of the romantic beauty of the myth in this strangely pragmatic reconstruction.

Local Birds (2001) features people from the rural community of Allenheads in Northumberland performing birdsong in their sitting rooms, sheds and cars. They are singing along to a slowed down recording of birdsong common to the area, but the footage has then been speeded up so that not only their voices but their mannerisms imitate the fluttering and twitching movements of a red grouse or a meadow pipit.

Although imitating birds, the participants have commented that the essential human characteristics of their friends are exaggerated by the performance. The act of attempting to be like another creature reveals the participants' personalities such that the film becomes an accurate, amusing and affectionate series of portraits of individuals in their natural habitat.

Steps a human could take to become an animal or bird

Fox

1. First go down on your hands and knees
2. Buy a mask
3. Place your tail on yourself
4. Practice your howls
5. Practice hiding behind rocks
6. Drive to a shop and buy some ears
7. Get some brown trousers
8. You have to learn to catch a rabbit
9. Dig a hole in a wood and live in it

Crocodile

1. Fix plastic legs onto thighs
2. Get next to a river and bask with mouth open
3. Then stay there

GoldenEagle

1. Climb up ladder
2. Tie rope around yourself
3. Lean forward with arms back
4. Start flapping arms and jump off branch.

From a children's workshop based on Coates' billboard image in the forest (Grizedale 2000) devised by Jenny Brownrigg

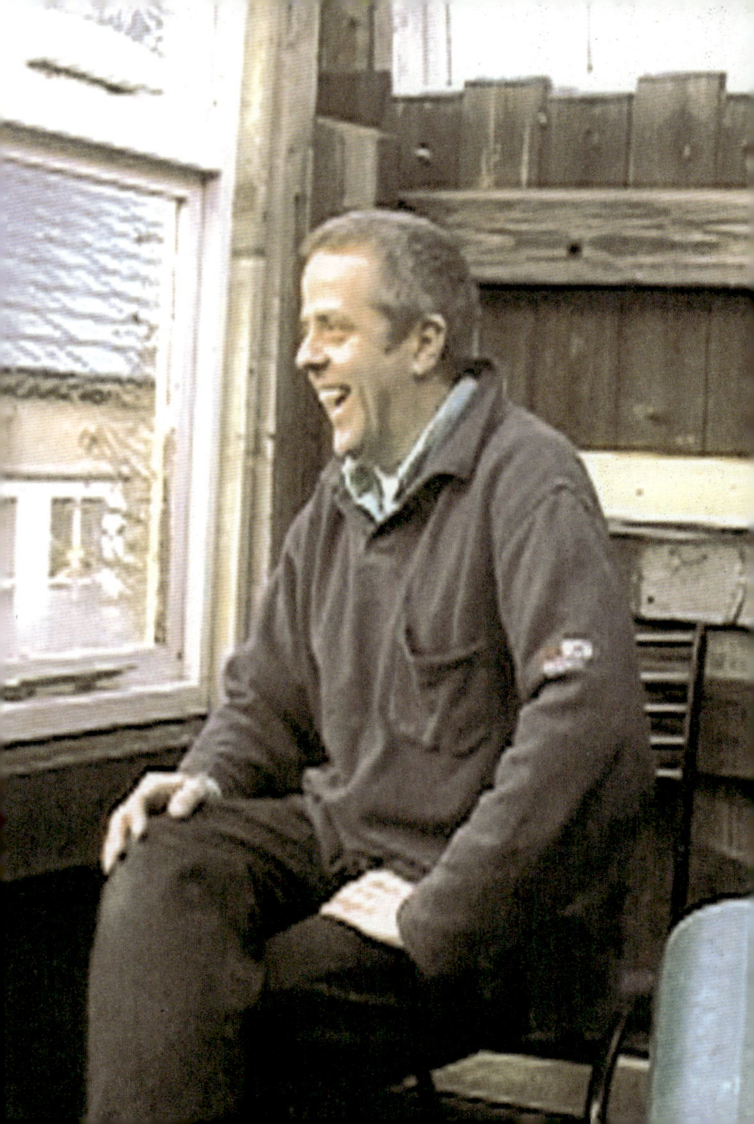

'Very ordinary women - the type you would spot in a supermarket'

Cindy Sherman 2003

Cindy Sherman

It is characteristic of Cindy Sherman's work that her own features are concealed in order to create her fictional characters, but her series of 'Untitled' portraits (2000) introduce a second layer of disguise. The thick make-up, prosthetics and perky poses fail to conceal the deterioration of the women's bodies as they face the aging process.

The style of the photographs, the monochrome background and the choice of head and torso shot, imitate that of the professional photography studio. These women have chosen to have their photograph taken and they are determined to look their best, only to reveal their futile attempts to perpetuate youth.

Sherman has always used the conventions of pop culture imagery to dramatise contemporary femininity. These women once epitomised the glamourous and fashionable ideal promoted by movies, advertising, and magazines but are now faced with using artificial means to maintain a positive self image.

Cindy Sherman was born in the USA in 1954 and now lives in New York

Image:
Cindy Sherman
Untitled # 360, 2000
Colour print
Courtesy the artist and Metro Pictures

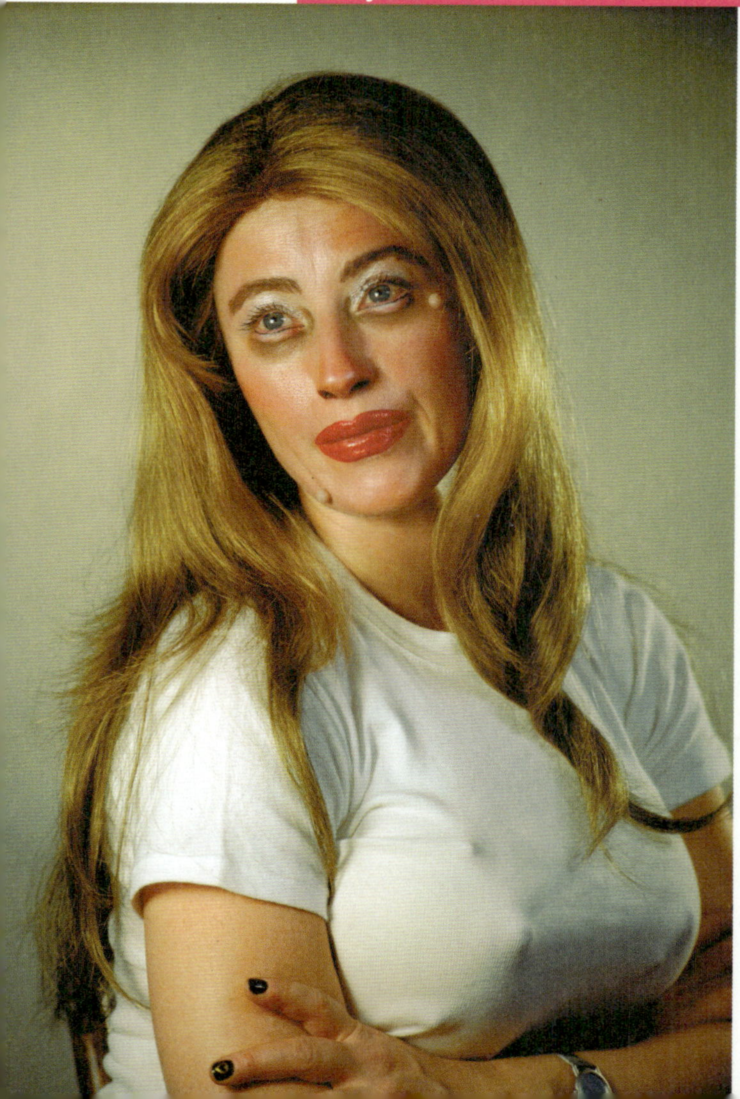

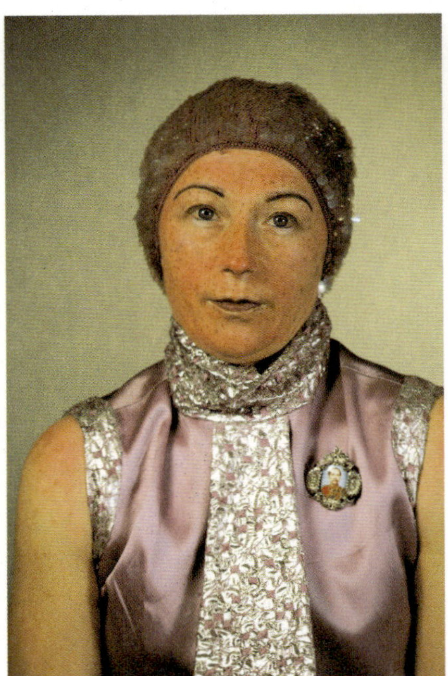

Image:
Cindy Sherman
Untitled # 351, 2000
Colour print
Courtesy the artist
and Metro Pictures

'Truth is identical with the surface, which hides nothing, covers no secret - everything else is a lie:' Carla Schulz-Hoffman, 1991, published by Kunsthalle Basel 1991

'I'd like people to fantasise about this person's life or what they're thinking or what's inside their head' Cindy Sherman 2003

Gillian Wearing

'It is as if we don a mask to unmask something, or someone else.' John Slyce, Contemporary no.55

We are all fascinated by other people's secrets. Gillian Wearing's work is compelling because it exposes feelings and experiences most of us would want to hide. However, as viewers we feel licensed to listen to these shocking admissions because the mystery individuals freely volunteer these stories and seem to find relief in telling them to a stranger.

Gillian Wearing placed an advert in Time Out magazine: *Confess all on video. Don't worry you will be in disguise. Intrigued? Call Gillian.* Her respondents were real people and the expectation is that we, as viewers, will be party to a confidence. The fact that they are disguised encourages us to believe the truth of these men's confessions because we recognise the freedom allowed by anonymity.

Wearing creates video and photographic work which sympathetically offers a glimpse of the shocking and tragic lives of ordinary but marginalised British people. She is influenced by the techniques of documentary film and confessional television, a genre which has grown dramatically since this artwork was made in 1994 to satisfy the TV audience's interest in the secret lives and behaviour of 'real people'

Gillian Wearing was born in 1963 in Birmingham, now lives in London

‘Masculine? Feminine? But it depends on the situation. Neuter is the only gender that always suits me.’ Claude Cahun

Claude Cahun

Claude Cahun was born in France in 1894 and died in Jersey in 1954

Image:
Claude Cahun
Self Portrait,
1927
Photograph
Courtesy Jersey Heritage Trust

Cahun’s extraordinary series of images of herself show a woman who felt at liberty to explore a wide range of identities despite the restrictions of her circumstances. Unwilling to be catagorised, she created a slippery and ambiguous personal image that is still fresh, over 50 years later. A woman who chooses to shave her hair is as revolutionary today as in 1920 and it is a testament to the quality of Cahun’s work that it remains so relevant.

For Claude Cahun, disguise was part of both her life and art. Born in France as Lucy Schwob, she adopted the more androgynous sounding name Claude Cahun and whilst in Paris in the 1920s lived with her partner Suzanne Malherbe. She became involved in the artistic and intellectual life of the Surrealists, frequenting journalistic and theatrical circles, but never exhibited her work during her lifetime.

In 1937 the couple moved to Jersey and combined creative with Resistance activities. Not only did Cahun impersonate a German officer in writing texts but also infiltrated German gatherings and outposts to distribute her flyers: dressing for both practical and political ends.

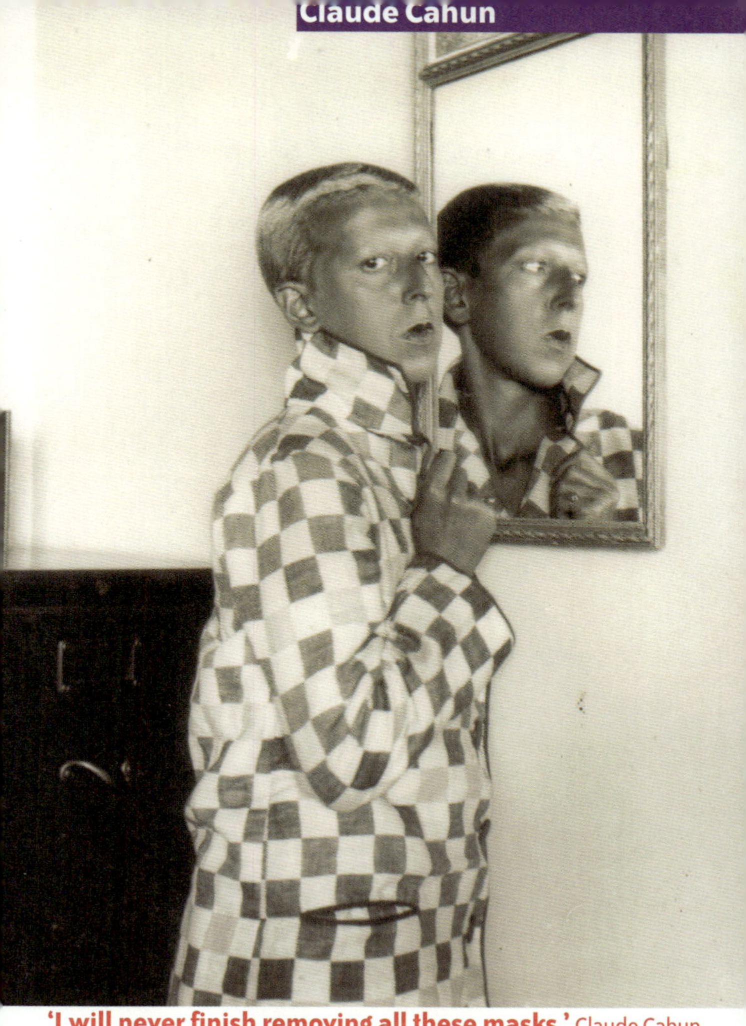

'I will never finish removing all these masks.' Claude Cahun

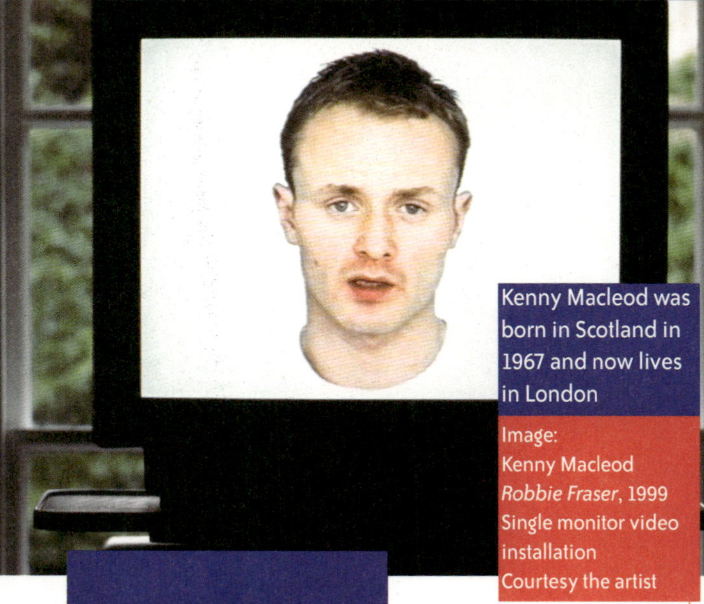

Kenny Macleod was born in Scotland in 1967 and now lives in London

Image:
Kenny Macleod
Robbie Fraser, 1999
Single monitor video installation
Courtesy the artist

Kenny Macleod

Everything about the appearance of this fresh-faced conventional young man, even the artist's well-spoken Scottish accent, prepares us to trust 'Robbie Fraser'. The white, neutral background and head shot recalls a video diary and indicates that some intimate disclosure awaits us. The information, feelings and opinions that gradually unfold initially satisfy our curiosity until he begins his introduction again and recounts a contradictory story. Key narrative elements such as his sexual identity, living arrangements, age and family background shift throughout the 16 stories leaving the viewer with nothing but the realisation that 'Robbie Fraser' reserves the right to be exactly who he claims to be.

Lies, fiction and truth become impossible to distinguish in the world of Robbie Fraser but his work also reflects a wider social reality. Words and text can create a disguise as successfully as visual transformation.

Hello, my name is Robbie Fraser. I'm 28 and I live in south west London. I moved to London in 1990 when I was 22, after completing a degree at the University of Edinburgh. My parents and my two brothers still live in Aberdeen, which is where I was born. They find it expensive to travel to London, and I don't often have the time to visit them in Aberdeen, so we rarely see one another. However I try to keep in touch by telephone as much as I can, because I think close family ties are so important don't you think?

Hello, my name is Robbie Fraser. I moved into my new house in south west London about 3 years ago. It's a very nice one bedroomed flat on the ground floor with a garden to the back, and bit by bit I have been furnishing as much as my income will allow. Now that I've reached thirty I feel much more settled after spending thirteen years sharing with others. It's great just to go home and to be completely alone. I can spread myself out as much as I please, and be as anti-social as I like without offending anyone.

Hello, my name is Robbie Fraser. In November 1996 I met my boyfriend who I now live with. He's two years older than me, and works as a broker in the City. I'm still not sure whether I want to spend the rest of my life with him and we have our ups and downs, but I think being in a relationship is better than living on my own. Although I enjoy my own company, I did sometimes get lonely. Living together can be difficult especially if, like me, you're not used to sharing space with a partner.

Transcript of part of 'Robbie Fraser'

Yasumasa Morimura

To introduce Morimura as a 'renowned male Japanese contemporary artist' uses a kind of categorisation that his images contradict. His complex self-portraits present a persona that is neither entirely man nor woman, Western nor Eastern, contemporary or historic.

Angels descending the stairs is part of Morimura's *Art History* series in which he replaces his own face with those of the main protagonists of famous oil paintings by Leonardo da Vinci, Rembrandt, Frida Kahlo and Cindy Sherman amongst many others. This work is based on 'The Golden Stairs' by Sir Edward Burne-Jones 1880 (TATE).

Like many of the artists in the exhibition, Morimura's disguise is deliberately ineffective. The fact that his big nose and Asian features are clearly visible within a famous image gives the work its sense of unease and ambiguity. This complexity reflects the artist's feelings about the multiple influences and experiences that contribute to his personal identity.

Morimura has been strongly influenced by Western culture but Japanese cultural tradition is also a strong element in his work. His adoption of the female image echoes the Japanese tradition of Kabuki theatre in which male actors play female roles

Yasumasa Morimura was born in Japan in 1951and now lives in Osaka

Image:
Yasumasa Morimura
Angels descending the stairs, 1991
Collection of Gallery Oldham

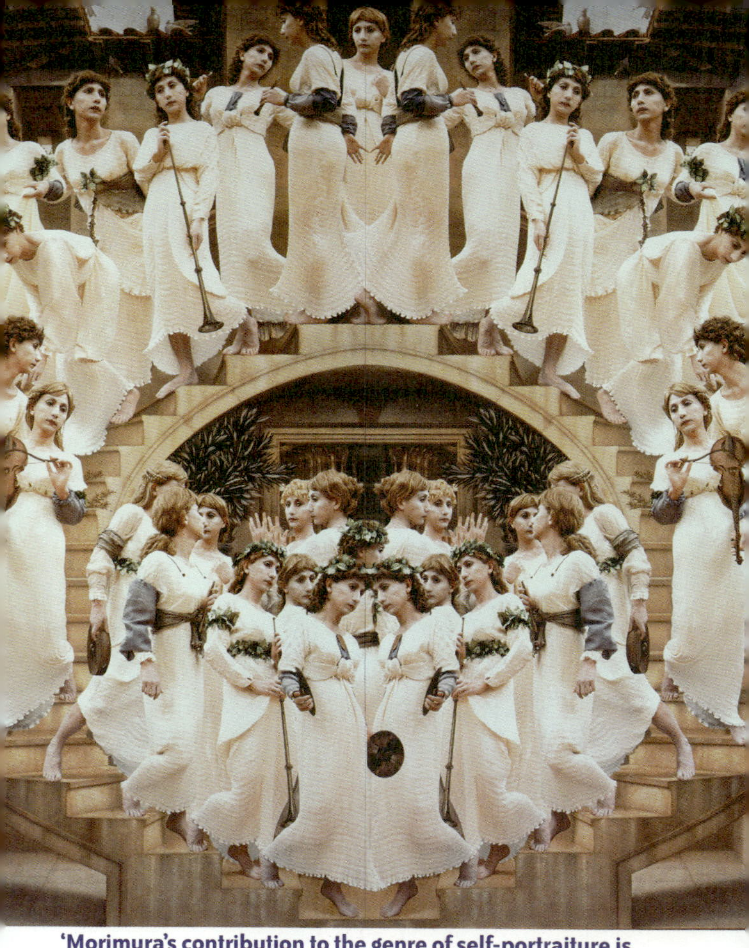

'Morimura's contribution to the genre of self-portraiture is substantial. He approaches it not only as a revelation of who he is, but as an exploration of the limitless possibilities to be whatever he wants' Lynn Gumpert in 'Art in America'

Nikki S Lee

Nikki S Lee's work demonstrates how prepared we all are to accept people at 'face value'. Lee appears in every photograph but her successful disguises make her hard to spot. Her images are not staged for the occasion of her photographs but represent moments in the artist's long term relationship with a community of people. Of all the artists in *Disguise*, it is Nikki S Lee who demonstrates the most extreme transformation by adopting a disguise for a period of months as she develops friendships and becomes accepted by one of the many different social groups which surround her in New York.

Although she painstakingly selects appropriate clothing and studies the behaviour of the group before approaching them, Lee's disguise is not a deception. She explains to her new companions that she is an artist and what her project involves. We can see from the familiar, comfortable demeanour of her new friends that they harbour no suspicion and have accepted her because she fits in.

Lee's experience as an immigrant from Seoul in South Korea informs her understanding and ability to adapt to different social and cultural environments. She brings to her art an Asian holistic view of the self, constantly defined by a fluctuating set of relationships with other people. In contrast, she feels that Westerners think of their identity as a unitary thing, ideally expressed through the manifestation of a single authentic persona no matter what the context.

Nikki S Lee was born in South Korea in 1970 and now lives in New York

Image
The Seniors Project (12), 1999
The Hip Hop Project (2), 2001

Fujiflex print

'Changing myself is part of my identity'

Nikki S Lee

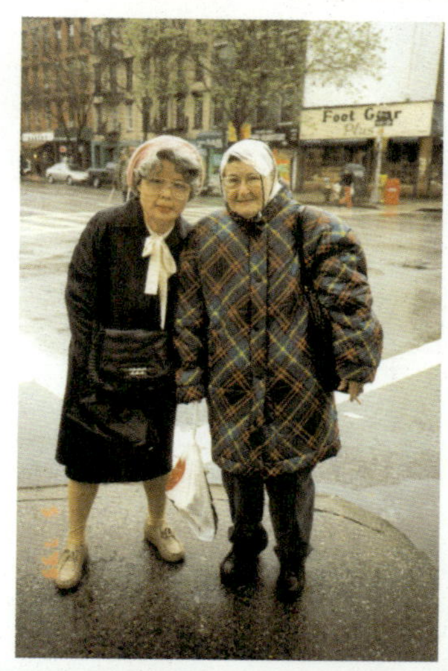

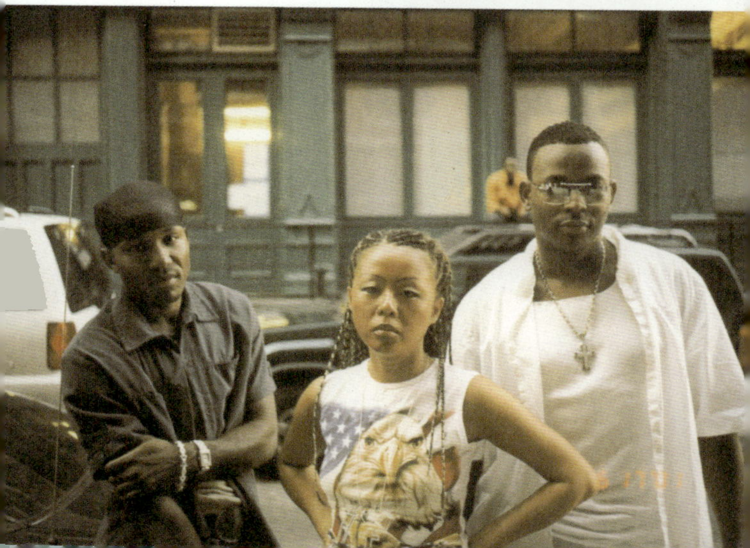

Events

Family Workshop
Activities for all on the theme of disguise.
Thursday 19 February 1.00 -3.00.
Free drop-in event for children of all ages with carer.
Education Studios.

Family Workshop
A joint event to celebrate Manchester Museum's *Transformations* and our *Disguise* exhibition. Mask-making at Manchester Museum; creating new identities at the Gallery. Invent a new set of credentials and id cards, have your photograph and finger prints taken.
Sunday 7 March 12 noon-3.00.
Free drop-in event for children 5 years and upwards with carer.

Exhibition Talk - Claude Cahun
Art historian Kristine von Oehsen gives an illustrated introduction to Claude Cahun's life and work with specific reference to the work on display.
Saturday 20 March 3.00 - 4.00.
Free ticket talk. Please book.

In Character
Inspired by Disguise and Great Expectations at the Royal Exchange, watch an actor transform himself into character, try it for yourself, using script excerpts, props and roleplay.
Sunday 4 April 1.00 - 3.30.
Free drop-in family event.

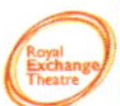

Family event - Birdcall...sounds like...
How do you disguise your own voice and call like a bird? Taking inspiration from Marcus Coates' video Local Birds, come and try your own bird call or make a bird head.
Wednesday 14 April & Thursday 15 April 1.00 - 3.00, Free drop-in family event for children of all ages with carer.

Adult Workshop - Portrait Painting
Inspired by the Disguise, work in paint from the portrait model provided.
Saturday 24 April 10.00 - 4.00.
Ticket event, £16, please book.

Artist's Talk - Laura Ford
The artist discusses her work with Dr David Lomas, University of Manchester School of Art and Archaeology.
Saturday 8 May 2.00 - 3.00.
Free ticket event, please book.

Make up and Wig Demonstrations
How do you disguise yourself convincingly? Professional demonstrations on applying theatrical make-up and dressing wigs. A chance to try them for yourself.
Saturday 22 May 1.00 - 4.00.
Free drop-in family event.

Digital Disguise
Harriet Clarke, Artist-In-Residence, runs a series of photo studio sessions for you to question your own image and disguise yourself to be photographed and added to our participatory piece in the exhibition.
Saturday & Sunday 22 & 23, 29 & 30 May 5 & 6 June 1.00 - 4.00.
Free drop-in event.

Disguise is an exhibition of artwork by 12 international and UK artists. It demonstrates a thematic link between a number of contemporary artists and connects them with artists from earlier in the twentieth century. The project includes an exhibition and site-specific commission by Laura Ford for the entrance hall of Manchester Art Gallery.
Manchester Art Gallery's Creative Consultants Youth Board (age 15 - 23) have assisted with the presentation of the exhibition. Creative Consultants is part of en-vision, an action-research pilot programme set up by engage to tackle the barriers between galleries and young people.
Disguise has also inspired artwork by groups from Manchester Schools and NCH The Children's Charity groups as part of Manchester City Galleries' *Image and Identity* project. The exhibition includes the *Disguise* 'lounge' - a place to relax, find out about the art and make comments via mobile phone text to our plasma screen.

Arts & Business NW, New Partners has made an incentive investment in this project.

Arts & Business *New Partners*

MAINSTREAM

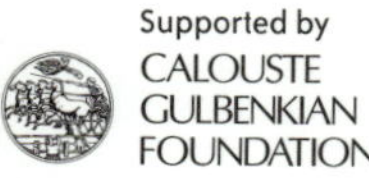

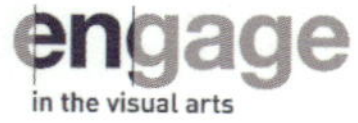

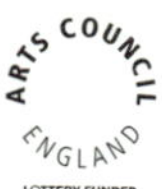

Manchester City Galleries would like to thank the following for their involvement in *Disguise:* Fergus Greer; Jersey Heritage Trust; Marcus Coates; Laura Ford; Houldsworth Gallery; Nikki S Lee; Leslie Tonkonow Artists + Projects; Kenny Macleod; Magnum Photos; Gallery Oldham; Prof Dr Thomas Olbricht; Arts Council Collection, Hayward Gallery London; students from the Manchester University Centre for Museology: Peter Brook, Nancy Lu, Ben Whittaker and all Manchester City Galleries staff involved in the project.

Virginia Tandy
Director of Manchester City Galleries

Manchester City Galleries Disguise Project Team: Denise Bowler; Curator, Formal Education, Fiona Corridan, Development Officer; Natasha Howes, Curator (Exhibitions and Displays); Morrigan Ellis, Project Co-ordinator (Image & Identity); Kim Gowland, Communications Manager; Marie Knudsen, Assistant Curator (Exhibitions and Displays); Pauline Maguire, Designer; Odile Masia Visitor Services Assistant; Claire McDade, Curator: Outreach; Emma Poulter, Art Gallery Trainee; Zoe Renilson, Public Programmes Curator; Seok-Joo Rhee, Conservator; Caroline Turner, Visitor Services Officer; Tim Wilcox Principal Curator (Exhibitions and Displays); Dawn Yates, Marketing Manager; Val Young, Development Manager; Manchester Art Gallery Creative Consultants Youth Board

Manchester Art Gallery
Mosley St
Manchester
M2 3JL
Tel + 44 (0) 161 235 8888
Fax + 44 (0) 161 235 8899
Textphone 0161 235 8893
www.manchestergalleries.org
Opening Hours Tuesday - Sunday 10.00 - 5.00
Closed Mondays except Bank Holidays

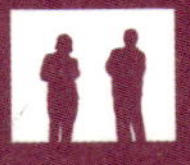
Manchester Art Gallery

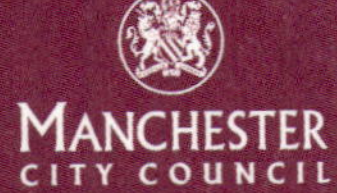

A Manchester City Galleries Exhibition

Led by Catherine Dickinson

Designed by Pauline Maguire, Designer, Manchester City Galleries

Cover: Embroidery by Simon Seabright, Logo artwork by Vincent Kelly

Printed by Andrew Kilburn Print Services on Crusade Offset using typeface Bailey Sans

Distributed by Cornerhouse Publications

ISBN 0 90167 365 X